Etsy –
The Book to Success

Become a successful Etsy shop owner with self-made products, jewelry, and second-hand items on an online platform with more than 20 M. customers.

Olav Kalt

Bibliografische Information der Deutschen Nationalbibliothek:

Die Deutsche Nationalbibliothek verzeichnet diese Publikation in der Deutschen Nationalbibliografie; detaillierte bibliografische Daten sind im Internet über http://dnb.dnb.de abrufbar.

Herstellung und Verlag: BoD –
Books on Demand, Norderstedt

ISBN: 978-3-7526-4088-5

Introduction

By using this book, you accept this disclaimer in full.

No advice

The book contains information. The information is not advice and should not be treated as such.

No representations or warranties

To the maximum extent permitted by applicable law and subject to section below, we exclude all representations, warranties, undertakings and guarantees relating to the book.

Without prejudice to the generality of the foregoing paragraph, we do not represent, warrant, undertake or guarantee:

- that the information in the book is correct, accurate, complete or non-misleading.

- that the use of the guidance in the book will lead to any particular outcome or result.

Limitations and exclusions of liability

The limitations and exclusions of liability set out in this section and elsewhere in this disclaimer: are subject to section 6 below; and govern all liabilities arising under the disclaimer or in relation to the book, including liabilities arising in contract, in tort (including negligence) and for breach of statutory duty.

We will not be liable to you in respect of any losses arising out of any event or events beyond our reasonable control.

We will not be liable to you in respect of any business losses, including without limitation loss of or damage to profits, income, revenue, use, production, anticipated savings, business, contracts, commercial opportunities or goodwill.

We will not be liable to you in respect of any loss or corruption of any data, database or software.

We will not be liable to you in respect of any special, indirect or consequential loss or damage.

Exceptions

Nothing in this disclaimer shall: limit or exclude our liability for death or personal injury resulting from negligence; limit or exclude our liability for fraud or fraudulent misrepresentation; limit any of our liabilities in any way that is not permitted under applicable law; or exclude any of our liabilities that may not be excluded under applicable law.

Severability

If a section of this disclaimer is determined by any court or other competent authority to be unlawful and/or unenforceable, the other sections of this disclaimer continue in effect.

If any unlawful and/or unenforceable section would be lawful or enforceable if part of it were deleted, that part will be deemed to be deleted, and the rest of the section will continue in effect.

Law and jurisdiction

This disclaimer will be governed by and construed in accordance with Swiss law, and any disputes relating to this disclaimer will be subject to the exclusive jurisdiction of the courts of Switzerland.

Inhaltsverzeichnis

Introduction

More and more guides with the topic »How you can become a millionaire in 90 days« are published. Hardly any of these is worth the electricity that the e-book needs to show the content. The dream of big money, if possible, yesterday and in any case without any effort, appears to be spreading more and more.

In fact, there are individual cases, people who very quickly became very rich on the internet. That happens about as frequently as people who stumble over a pot of gold during a walk in the woods or who win the super jackpot of the year in Lotto.

Dreaming is allowed and perhaps even relaxing, but those who build their plan for the future on it should already start looking for an application form for the social assistance office.

The internet is, in fact, a wonderful place for a part-time income or to secure oneself a whole existence. But fact with that is, that one needs to work hard in order to achieve that. As every form of self-deployment, also a (part-time) internet self-deployment demands a lot of effort and excellent performance, especially in the early days.

After my first book about my experiences with the American Fiverr.com platform, on which many sellers earn thousands of euros and more monthly, in this book, I want to introduce to you the Etsy marketplace, on which 30 m. items are up for sale and almost 1.5 m. sellers come upon 20 m. of potential customers.

What is interesting about the Etsy marketplace is a very clear, to my knowledge, unique positioning (at least for a platform with that amount of customers) on homemade products and vintage items, that have to be at least 20 years old. You do not find just any mass-produced goods or cheap junk on there. Also the fact that the majority of suppliers and customers is female makes the platform a »special place in the WWW«.

Now it is undoubtedly not everyone's cup of tea to offer self-made items or basement and jumble troves online; but those who have a certain creativity (or an overfilled basement), can earn good money, attract a regular clientele and especially also meet interesting people through exchanges with other sellers with the help of the strong community approach of Etsy.

Visit the page and get inspired, whether you »only« become a customer or a seller - those who do not know the page, certainly miss out on something.

Enjoy browsing,

Yours, Olav Kalt

What is Etsy?

Etsy introduces itself on its website in the following way:

Etsy is a marketplace where people around the world connect, both online and offline, to make, sell and buy unique goods.

The heart and soul of Etsy is our global community: the creative entrepreneurs who use Etsy to sell what they make or curate, the shoppers looking for things they can't find anywhere else, the manufacturers who partner with Etsy sellers to help them grow, and the Etsy employees who maintain and nurture our marketplace.

On the website the following numbers are presented:

Founded	2005
Employees	717
Items for sale	32 m.
Active sellers	1.4 m.
Active buyers	20.4 m.
Annual gross merchandise sales	1.93 bn. $

This is undoubtedly a platform that must be taken seriously and whose dimensions are gigantic compared to most European providers.

Providers, again and again, are amazed at their successes. Several providers that I know of have started their first attempts on that platform after the items that they had found on attics could not be sold on other platforms or only changed hands for a quite »symbolic price«. Many providers realized that they were able to charge considerably better prices for well-presented items on Etsy. With that, especially those sellers are successful, who do not simply run a »shop«, but who really stand behind it with blood, sweat, and tears and thus also use other social media channels, such as Pinterest or Facebook in order to get additional attention and to also achieve customer loyalty.

Regardless, of whether you are an »internet old-timer« or never have sold anything on the internet: Etsy offers a very easy entry to get successful quickly. This book will help you with that.

Owning an Etsy shop can present a fundamental change for you. Especially people that work creatively and mechanically, often experience that is extremely difficult to even realize the cost price with what they do. An important reason for that is that many creative people do not have access to a sufficient number of potential customers. With an active customer base of more than 20 m. people worldwide, Etsy provides a remedy.

No matter how exotic your works might be (as long as the ydo not violate the guidelines of Etsy); every style and make finds fans on here and many a »hobby artist« was able to develop a sufficient (additional) income after some time, which allowed him to partially or entirely live off his works. The same applies to passionate junk dealers.

Who buys on Etsy?

According to a study from 2012, about 67% of the buyers on Etsy are female. Many of them have a level of education, are childless and have a good income. If one wants to probe the customers of Etsy a bit more in detail, it is a good method to look at the most successful shop operators of Etsy in 2014:

Shop	Number of sales	Main topic of the Shop
ThinkPink-Bows	119180	Hairbands
Rivermil-lEmbroidery	104220	Embroidery

Thevel-vetacorn	96605	Knitwear and crochet fashion
beanforest	96106	Cups and pins with funny motifs
ThreeBird-Nest	90726	Accessories
signa-turetshirts	81862	T-Shirts with special imprints
zenthreads	81480	Imprinted textiles
PrettyGraf-ikdesign	74556	digital stamps and backgrounds

col-lageOrama	67472	Imprints on old dictionary pages
norajane	66813	Handmade stamps
OnceUpon ATimeTu-Tus	64096	Tutus and accessories
PurplePos-sum	61325	Birthday dresses for children
ru-bylovedesig ns	61008	Baby and School albums
applelatte	60359	Jewelry
bragging-bags	59848	Items for weddings

MayaHoney	58585	Czech Jewelry pearls made of glass or similar material
DistinctlyIvy	57619	Personalized jewelry
The-SageGoddess	56514	Supplies for ritual magic (stones, candles, etc.)

This list is not about revenues, but about the amount of ordered items! The sales vary based on the offered items. If you, for example, calculate with about 20 Euros average cost per item with ThreeBirdNest, you end up with a revenue of about 1.8 m. euros. The probability that these accessories are produced by one single person at their kitchen table is not very high. But a restriction to handmade items does not mean that the seller has to produce them all on his own. But there are, in fact, several sellers that offer either their own works or, for example, the works of a group of craftsmen and artists.

The figures show that a lot of money is spent on that platform and also that a good income can be generated with good quality and interesting offers.

In addition to sellers from the US, there are also companies from South Korea, Slovakia, Israel, Italy, Canada, Australia and other countries in the list of the top 100 sellers. Many successful sellers also come from German-speaking countries or other European countries. It is especially important to many sellers that every seller can also define to where he can ship. Thus, nobody needs to shy away from any tariff subjects or the like.

Bases for successes on Etsy

Before you now start to set up an own Etsy shop, you should take some topics into account in order to successfully get started later on.

Many Etsy sellers achieve monthly sales of a few Euros as pocket money, whereas others achieve far more than 1000 euros of sales or even enough to cover both the production costs as well as their subsistence. Every seller can decide that for himself.

A seller must, in any case, be aware that building a clientele on Etsy also requires time as well as some strategic considerations and that it does in general not happen »over

night«, by accident. Here, success is connected to work, too.

Get to know Etsy

Before you start planning your own shop,
you should look around on Etsy:

- Which other sellers are there in your work area?

- What do these sellers offer?

- What do they charge for their products?

- How much do they sell? (Can be estimated by looking at the published figures »founding« and »Amount of sales«. Also, an important number is the number of admirers.)

- How do the sellers present their products?

- How do they describe them?

- How could that be done in a better way?

- How are your asking prices compared to existing prices (Good offers that

are presented positively do not neces-
sarily have to be the cheapest in order
to get bought.)

- To where do the sellers ship?

- Which offers do the sellers make that
  you could also offer as a supple-
  mental offering?

- Which offers are lacking with some
  sellers where you could perhaps fill in
  gaps?

Write down your findings and take them into
account during the various stages of the pro-
ject as a source of inspiration.

Besides that, familiarize yourself with the
navigation and the search for the marketplace and also make a few orders - of course,

you can cancel before the actual »purchase«, unless you want to purchase the items. It is simply important to develop a feeling for the platform, so that you are able to determine, based on that, whether your future shop could exist on there.

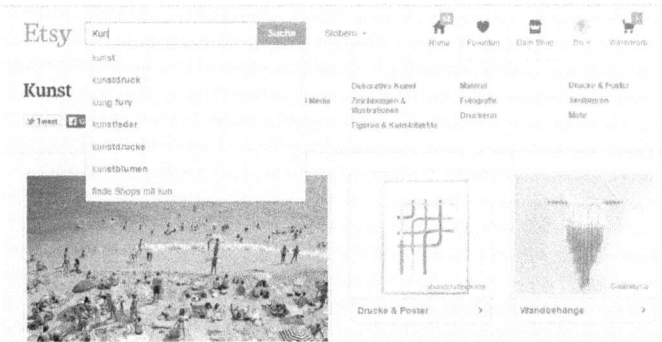

It also makes sense to read through the sales manual of Etsy. It contains a variety of very interesting and helpful information for (prospective) sellers. You can find the sales manual on here:

https://www.etsy.com/de/seller-handbook

Set goals for yourself

If you do not only want to operate on Etsy as an alongside hobby, but rather wish to a achieve a regular income with the help of Etsy in the medium to long run, it is in my experience, in general, of importance to define clear goals. As trite as this »wisdom« may be.

Many companies still live for the day and have the goal to achieve »as much as possible«. That is not a goal, but rather a permanent excuse to not be embarrassed for not having achieved a goal. Those who set goals, match them and work on achieving something. Depending on the set goals, one will take certain measures and make certain decisions.

Most Etsy entrepreneurs have (as in other areas, too) defined clear goals in written form in regard to revenues and amount of orders.

Well defined goals always follow the SMART rule. They are:

- Specific - it is clear what wants to be achieved.

- Measurable - it is defined how it is measured whether the goal has been achieved.

- Ambitious - Goals that you achieve »easily« do not challenge you and do not get you anywhere.

- Realistic - unrealistic dream goals will not help you to »bite yourself through« hard times. They mean permanent demotivation because neither goals nor intermediate goals are achieved.

- Terminated - Goals always have a time at which they have to be (at the latest) achieved.

It makes sense to stagger goals (resp. break them down). With that, it can be a reasonable goal to achieve a revenue of 100 euros in the first month. For the following month, you perhaps define a doubling of the revenue or an additional amount of minimum offers... Depending on your goals, the figures can vary greatly.

Clear, achievable, but still challenging goals help you to actually achieve them and if you write your goals down and compare the current status at least weekly with the monthly goals, you have the possibility to think about an appropriate measure when you are trailing behind with the plan at any time.

Sell what customers want

Many sellers spend a lot of time on convincing people to buy what they have to offer. Of course that is to you. I personally remember a friend who painted frightening pictures which he put into self-made, very creative and matching frames and tried to sell the product.

In fact, there were only extremely few buyers; an art dealer bought a picture once in a while. My friend was already about to give up with his art because he could by far not live from what he earned with the one regular customer. Fortunately, the two of them started talking, in particular when my friend wanted to tell his client that he would give up on art und wanted to do something »solid«.

He learned from the customer that he separated the images from the frame. The images still lay around at his home in a folder, but the frames were pried out of his hands and achieved much higher prices than the pictures within the frames. Today, my friend produces frames. He only draws for private pleasure nowadays and from time to time he exhibits them in a small circle. The frames are still pried out of his hands.

Of course it might not be nice for an artist to learn that his art is judged differently by other people. But there are undoubtedly various possibilities to handle such a situation. If you want to sustainably earn money with your products, you should, at least, think about on what the visitors of your page would spend money.

This should in no case be interpreted in the way that you were forced to literally create copies of successful items. A major advantage of Etsy is that interested persons can be found for almost every topic. Though it makes sense to use all possible sources in order to find out what sells well on Etsy because you will, at least, be able to make fundamental decisions. For that I will present you three methods:

- Ask Etsy

- Ask Google

- Ask Craftscount.com

Even though Etsy does not publish the sales figures and revenues of its members, there are some very important signs for finding out whether a product attracts interest on Etsy. A first sign is undoubtedly the number of customers in a shop. In combination with the period of time that the shop is already active, sales figures can be estimated. Besides that, it is also worthwhile to directly look at the single items. On Etsy (as on many other platforms) customers rate their sellers. This has many positive aspects for you as a potential seller. Firstly, you can reason the amount of interest in an item from the amount of feedback. Perhaps even more important is the possibility to recognize wishes and suggestions in feedback for the product by the customer. This provides you with the possibility to, already in advance, involve these feedbacks in your planning.

Benutzerdefinierte Kalligrafie Grafik, bis zu 10 Wortern Ihrer Wahl, Art Print, Hand-gelettert von Tinte und Anne

★ ★ ★ ★ ★

I am very happy with my order! Krista does beautiful work! Thank you!

🌐 Übersetzen

Bewertet von magplepony am 07. Jul 2015

2 Custom Prints

★ ★ ★ ★ ★

Wonderful prints, and the seller was great about working with me to create what I was looking for

🌐 Übersetzen

Bewertet von Allison am 26. Juni 2015

Custom Gift Tags

★ ★ ★ ★ ★

Easy purchase, and the tags turned out so beautifully. Thank you!

🌐 Übersetzen

Bewertet von Maurie Bretcher am 15. Juni 2015

Custom Calligraphy Print, 10+ words of your choice, Art Print, Modern Calligraphy, hand lettered by Ink and Anne

★ ★ ★ ★ ★

beautiful work, great interaction with seller, would buy from again

🌐 Übersetzen

The search suggestions of Etsy in the search bar provide you with another sign. If you enter your keyword in there, Etsy will show you the most searched keywords in which your word/ a part of your word is contained. The results can also change over time when other products become more current. Who today, for example, entered »watch«, got as search suggestions: »watch, watches, watchband, wood watch«. That can, depending on the product that you offer, be interesting in order to determine sales figures. This kind of search is also of interest at a later point in time when you have to define keywords for your product which also lead to a higher hit ratio in the Etsy search and thus to more sales if you integrate popular keywords in your shop and product description.

A wonderful possibility in order to find out which topics are searched on the internet, offers the advertising planner from Google Adwords. Even if you do not want to advertise on Google, a respective account is worthwhile. It is for free and can be created without obligation.

https://adwords.google.com/KeywordPlanner

**Google AdWords
Keyword-Planer**

Planen Sie Ihre Kampagnen im Suchnetzwerk
und erfahren Sie, wonach Ihre Kunden suchen.

In AdWords anmelden

Neue Ideen für Keywords und Anzeigengruppen finden

Der Keyword-Planer ist ein zentraler Ort, an dem Sie neue Kampagnen für das Suchnetzwerk erstellen oder bereits vorhandene Kampagnen erweitern können. Sie haben die Möglichkeit, nach Ideen für Keywords und Anzeigengruppen zu suchen, Verlaufsstatistiken anzusehen, die mögliche Leistung bestimmter Keywords abzurufen und sogar eine neue Keyword-Liste zu erstellen, indem Sie mehrere Listen mit Keywords miteinander kombinieren. Außerdem unterstützt Sie das kostenlose AdWords-Tool bei der Auswahl wettbewerbsfähiger Gebote und Budgets für Ihre Kampagnen.

Ob Einsteiger oder Experte in der Onlinewerbung – mit dem Keyword-Planer legen Sie den Grundstein für eine erfolgreiche Kampagne. Weitere Informationen

If you now chose »find out new keywords«, optionally based on your website, your products or on the basis of subjects that you enter, you can now get suggestions for keywords. The advantage with that is that you can also limit the search even more to the region or languages that are of interest to you.

The fact that Google also shows you how often found keywords of the region/ language... you named were found and how high the competition is. Keywords that nobody searches are no subjects for boards, whereas subjects with a high search frequency are suitable.

In the tools of Google Adwords, you can also find the selection: »Plan budget and call up keyword data«. Copy the found keywords into the search bar (separated by commas) and let Google show you which popularity the various terms have in their Google search.

Budget planen und Keyword-Daten abrufen

▼ Daten zum Suchvolumen und Trends abrufen

1. Option: Keywords eingeben

Haarband
Haarbänder
Kopfschmuck
Hut
Kappe

2. Option: Datei hochladen

Datei auswählen...

CSV- und TSV-Dateien sowie Textdateien zulässig Weitere Informationen

Ausrichtung [?]   Zeitraum [?]

Berlin   Durchschnittliche monatliche
                                   Suchanfragen anzeigen für:
Google   Letzte 12 Monate

Auszuschließende
Keywords

Suchvolumen abrufen

Interesting keywords are especially those for which there are many search requests, but little competition amongst the sellers. Here you have a lot of potential to stand out from the crowd. The best results always bring a keyword for which there are many search requests, but which nobody uses in their public image. Here you literally had 100% of the hits that contained your offer as a suggestion. This is undoubtedly an ideal case that can only be realized in very few cases.

	Durchschnittl. Suchanfragen pro Monat [?]	Wettbewerb [?]	
[~]	1.000	Mittel	
[~]	590	Hoch	
[~]	210	Mittel	
[~]	260	Hoch	
[~]	210	Hoch	
		Zeilen anzeigen: 30 ▼	

Also, the keywords that were found like this should be used for better traceability in the shop description and/or product description. With that, it should always be remembered that the texts for the customers should possibly be pleasant to read, Search engine optimization must therefore always only come second after customer and reader friendliness.

Ask Craftcount.com

Craftcount.com is a valuable source of information for learning how to best position your Etsy shop. Shops of sellers with more than 1000 sales are only registered if they apply for that. Because with that additional links are directed to their own job, most providers do that and the search results are, thus, accordingly significant.

Top Etsy Sellers

Top 10 Overall

Top 10 Handmade

Rank	Name	Sales	Rank	Name	Sales
1	BohemianFindings	530004			
2	cibeads	374290			
3	yummytreasures	328929			
4	shareliving	303100			
5	yadanabeads	299147			
6	EverLuxe	292173			
7	dimestoreemporium	290442			
8	happysupplies	284836			
9	nicoledebruin	262277			
10	MiniatureSweet	243882			

Particularly interesting for our purpose is the display top sellers by category. On there, you can find the most successful sellers for every category that exists on Etsy. If you look at the category in which you intended to sell, you can draw a conclusion on the competition based on the amount of listed shops and also on the potential based on the amount of sold items.

Look at the top 10 shops in your category. These do many things properly - in respect of winning customers. Make notes on the following aspects of every shop:

- How does it present itself (images, texts)?

- Which sections did he choose?

- What appeals to me?

- What can I learn from the provider?

- What do I not like?

- What can I perhaps do better?

- Which advantages do I have compared to the other seller (that can be products, prices, image quality, descriptions, delivery conditions and much else)?

- Which offers / niches can I fill that the provider does not offer?

Include this knowledge when setting up your own shop. With that, however, always note that it is not about copying the other person, but about getting the best out of your offer - especially on Etsy, the seller that stands behind an offer is an important success factor.

Set up your own Etsy shop

After you have now gotten an overview and also invested much time into planning and getting to know everything, let us now start creating your Etsy shop.

It should be your goal to positively impress visitors with your shop and to get them to visit it again and again. At the same time, the shop should stand out from many other shops so that it can be found easily. You achieve that mainly by putting up a clear profile on your shop. The convenience store, where you get a little bit of everything, will be appreciated less than a top specialist shop for one topic.

Market experiences have long ago demonstrated that, as well as the willingness of the customers to spend a bit more in moderation at the specialist than in the supermarket – if the product lies at their heart.

But because you always have the possibility do adjust and optimize things based on experience, you should not spend too much time on groundwork and details. Because during that time, you do not earn money and that is considerably less than what you would achieve with a bad shop.

The name

The first important decision that you need to make is the name of your shop. In the future, your customers will search for you with it. To secure the search success, you need to take some aspects into account:

- The shop name should be easy to remember and to write. If customers are neither capable of remembering nor writing the name, you thereby give away sales.

- Depending on where you want to ship, it can make sense to choose a term from a particular language. Those who see most potential in English-speaking areas should avoid purely German terms.

- Do not use a name that is branded or the like.

- Do not use names that are too similar to already existing shop's names.

- Consider the worldview of you target group and their standards when choosing the name.

- The shop name is a coherent term without spaces. You can distinguish several words with the help of using capitalization: e.g. »CandleShopBerlin«.

- Compose the shop name of not more than three words.

- When choosing the name prefer a term that is also searched for on Google and Etsy and thus brings you additional visitors.

The banner

The shop banner makes it easy to distinguish how much blood, sweat and tears a shop owner invested in his shop. It largely corresponds to the fittings of a real shop. That is where the shop visitors get their first impression from. It decides about whether the visitor will browse your shop or whether he will search for another one. As a seller on Etsy, one needs to be aware that one operates one's shop in a "shopping center" with more than 1 m. other shops.

Of course you can create the banner by your-self. The question with that is how good your respective skills are. An Etsy banner has dimensions of 760x100 pixels with a 72 dpi resolution. .Jpg, .png and .gif formats are accepted. It can be created with conventional graphic programs. Alternatively, there exist two online services that offer respective templates, that are for free or which can be used for a small amount of money.

http://www.etsybannergenerator.com/

Or

https://www.canva.com/create/ban-
ners/etsy-banners/

Alternatively, you can go to Fiverr.com and
let someone else create a banner for Etsy for
5 US$ for you.

Search Results for 'Etsy'

When creating a banner, you should consider the following aspects:

- The shop name is what is most important. It should be easily readable. Do not use special fonts which can only be deciphered by specialists.

- Colors, motifs, and design should fit the offered products.

- You should like the banner and it should »fit your personality«.

The avatar

The small image of the shop owner that appears at various points in the shop and item description is called an avatar. Most Etsy sellers use either a picture of themselves, a company logo or a picture that is connected to their shop for that.

It can be adjusted in the account settings in the profile settings.

In my opinion, it is a mistake to not show one's face. Especially with Etsy, the aspect »trust and personality« is important. Less important is the question of personal attractiveness or of meeting an ideal of beauty. People buy from people - and if you own a good picture of yourself on which you may even smile, then it is a good candidate for an avatar image.

The image has 75 pixels and is square. Although Etsy is able to adjust images, if you already upload a suitable one, you reduce the risk of blurring.

The shop title

The shop title is kind of the slogan or the brief description of your shop. If your shop, for example, is called »handmade fishing baits«, your shop title could be: »handmade fishing baits for fresh and salt water fish«. The title can be up to 66 characters long and can consist of letters and numbers. It can be adjusted in the settings. Because the title is also relevant for the search routines on Etsy and Google, it is worthwhile to also consider to include your chosen keywords.

The shop announcement

The announcements are used very differently in various shops. Some inform themselves about current special offers or new items on there, others describe their offer more precisely. Also possible are quotes from customer reviews or the like. Because only the first two lines are displayed (more, only if the customer clicks on it), you should be brief.

Your shop profile

People buy from people. Use the possibility to introduce yourself and your concerns to your customers. Of course you can also mention further links to your Pinterest or Facebook page. People buy (as already mentioned) from people, and with the kind of products that are offered on Etsy, the feeling of the customer of what is behind the offer is very important.

Shop Policies / GTC

Mention your sales principles in regard to delivery, return, reclamation, etc. People prefer to buy from shops with clear GTCs.

█████████ AGB

Willkommensgruß

Hereinspaziert! - Viele frische neue Designs von Miniblings!
Täglich kommen neue hinzu!

Zahlung

Hallo!

Wenn Sie überweisen möchten bitte auf

█████████████████

█████████████████████████████

Das Miniblings Team

Versand

Vielen Dank für Deinen Kauf bei Miniblings!
Wir versenden Deine Ware sofort nach Geldeingang.
Wir versenden 3-5 Mal pro Woche.

Versandzeiten

Deutschland: Der Versand erfolgt mit der PIN AG und der deutschen Post und
dauert 1-5 Werktage (meist 2-3)

Europa: 2-14 Tage
USA: 5-20 Tage
Welt: 5-30 Tage

(diese Zeiten sind ungefähre Schätzungen, wir können keine Garantie für eine
rechtzeitge Zustellung übernehmen, weil wir das nicht selber in der Hand haben.)

Das Miniblings-Team

Widerrufs- oder Rückgabebelehrung

Widerrufsrecht für Verbraucher
(Verbraucher ist jede natürliche Person, die ein Rechtsgeschäft zu Zwecken
abschließt, die überwiegend weder ihrer gewerblichen noch ihrer selbstständigen
beruflichen Tätigkeit zugerechnet werden kann.)

Widerrufsbelehrung

Widerrufsrecht
Sie haben das Recht, binnen vierzehn Tagen ohne Angabe von Gründen diesen

Welcome

In this section, you can welcome customers and draw attention to special possibilities, such as »custom-made« or the like, if necessary.

Payment

Inform your customers about the payment possibility via PayPal. Many people do not realize that they can also pay with credit and debit cards on PayPal without making a PayPal account for themselves. With that, you can reduce reservations.

Inform the customers about types of delivery, delivery firms, time to delivery and everything else that might be important to the customer in that context. If you for example re-use packaging, mention that as well, that also corresponds to the spirit of Etsy.

Another important aspect can be how you deal with orders if the delivery address is different from the PayPal address. Some suppliers only send to the address that is submitted on PayPal, whereas others use the delivery address that is mentioned on Etsy.

Cancellation or return policy

Enter the respective conditions on there. Note that – depending on the country in which you run your shop – also legal regulations apply, if necessary.

Further policies and FAQs

On there you can enter what is also of importance to your customers.

Social media connections

In your account settings, you can connect your account with Facebook, Google+ and Twitter. If you have an account for displaying your business activity or your works on any of these websites, it makes sense to include these in order to approach additional contacts and potential customers. Moreover, it can also have a positive effect on the building a customer community and on the customer loyalty.

Offering products

The price

Before you set out to arbitrarily post products on Etsy, you should also spend some time thinking and getting to know the market for the respective items. If there are other sellers that offer comparable products, two basic directions are possible.

a) You offer your products at a similar or a tendentially cheaper price because you are at a disadvantage compared to the better-known seller. With that strategy, the question is how attractive that is in the long run. At best, this strategy makes sense at the beginning to establish your reputation and should then gradually be abandoned.

b) I probably better strategy is always to provide the customer with more benefit than to be cheaper than the competition. For that, it is important to think about what brings the customer additional benefit based on feedback etc. If you make an obviously better offer, there is a good chance that people will pay a bit more for it than for a long-established seller.

Therefore, it is imaginable that seller with hand-knitted scarves leaves the choice of motif to the customer or that the seller offers a special gift packaging for giving away or that the seller of special baits additionally offers an e-book with the topic of how to optimally maintain or use the baits. The number of possibilities is unlimited.

Try different strategies and adjust the offers that do not sell well. For that, note which measures achieved which results. Such records can become the base for many successful offers over the time.

As possibilities for pricing the following aspects have been proven to be successful:

- Interviews: Ask friends and potential customers what the offered items are worth to them. With that, make sure that such responses should often be treated with caution. Who would say to a friend that what he has created with a lot of blood, sweat and tears over a period of time is at most worth a few cents?

- Comparison with other platforms. Find comparable products on different platforms, such as eBay. Note, however, that especially on eBay (auction where one wants to make a bargain) tendentially less is spent than on a platform like Etsy.

Besides the question of what the market is willing to pay for your product, there is a second, at least equally as important aspect that you need to consider for pricing. It is the question of your costs, These essentially consist of the following elements:

- Costs for the material

- Costs for advertisement and marketing (incl. costs for Etsy and PayPal).

- Costs for external services (e.g. if one work piece is manufactured by a service provider)

- Costs for packaging (packet, labels, ink)

- Your work performance for making, marketing, packaging, and shipping.

Proceed very professionally and really calculate everything, even the smallest cent amounts. An offer is not fun if you do not get any profit from it.

Because you do not only offer a single item, it is a good idea to offer a good mix of low and high-priced items. For that, also, look at various shops with comparable products and consider their mix and the products that are sold best. In any case, you should offer a wider range. In order to get an overview, it is advisable to search for the respective product in the search of Etsy and to then sort the shops based on price. With that, you get a good overview of offers from cheap (organize prices from low to high) to expensive (sorting of price vice versa).

Perhaps, you will find out that also sets are often offered in your category. This has the advantage that the effort of entering is focused and that is also much more fun to sell 3 fishing baits for 18 euros than one for 6. Of course this is very different with different product categories as well. Especially, when it comes to »art«, a set can also seem cheap and, therefore, reduce the trust in the product.

Which offers are especially successful

If one looks a bit around on Craft count, one will quickly discover that the most success-ful shops where all elements seem very pro-fessional and thorough from graphics over images up to completeness of the offer. You will not be able to afford everything of that at the beginning of your career on Etsy.

Artikeldetails

Erzähle der Welt von deinem Artikel und wie toll er ist.

Titel

Beschreibe deinen Artikel mit
Wörtern und Sätzen, die die Leute
bei ihrer Suche verwenden würden

Über diesen Artikel

| Wer hat es gemac... ▾ | Was ist es? ▾ | Wann wurde es ge... ▾ |

Erfahre mehr darüber, welche Art von
Artikeln auf Etsy erlaubt sind

Kategorie

Keine ▾

Preis

CHF

Beziehe Kosten für Materialien und
Arbeitszeit sowie sonstige
Geschäftsausgaben ein.

Stückzahl

1

Bei Mengen von mehr als 1 reduziere
wir den Artikel automatisch, bis er
ausverkauft ist. Dir wird jedes Mal
eine Einstellgebühr von €0.20 USD
berechnet.

Art

◉ Physisch ◯ Digital

Beschreibung

Mache die Liste gezielt auf dein
Produkt, deinen Shop und dich.
Neben zentralen Merkmalen, Maßen
und Vorschlägen zu
Verwendungszwecken kannst du
auch deinen Prozess und deine
Inspirationen beschreiben.

Artikel als Google-Suchergebnis ansehen Vorschau

Nevertheless, you should create professional offers from beginning on. That means that you upload good pictures. Several providers on eBay offer whole equipment with light tent and lights for only a little money. Of course that can be unnecessary, depending on the offered items. But in any case, pay attention to well-lit, clear images. Also detailed views and views from different perspectives can be promotional.

Regarding the images Etsy writes:

Use high-quality JPG-, PNG- or GIF-files, that are at least 570 px wide (we recommend 1000 px). Photo advice: Do not use flash.

In order to also optimize the images for search engines, you should label the images according to their offers. Google searches through all images and the probability to be shown and to win respective prospects is much higher when your image is called »fishing_bait.jpg« than when you label it »photo0001.jpg«. Because most people miss that aspect and because images have a better effect than only text, that strategy can achieve significant advantages.

The title

The title is what besides the image decides about whether a prospect looks at your product more precisely. You should pay attention to the following points:

- Create easily readable titles.

- Use clear titles on the base of which the prospect can find out what the offer is about.

- Use keywords in order to also get listed better by search engines of Etsy and Google.

- Vary the keywords and thus, increase the chance of being found. (To be precise, not every offer with the same keyword).

- Avoid meaningless adjectives such as »unique, seldom, rare, great, beautiful, decorative«.

- Let yourself inspire by successful sellers of your category.

- Avoid slang expressions.

Description

The following three questions in the input mask will be a bit special:

- Who made it?

- What is it?

- When was it made?

The questions are related to the rules of Etsy, which only allow handmade items, supply for making such items and vintage items to be offered.

Offered products can by the way also be digital. There is the possibility to offer handmade music, software, e-books, videos, games or something similar, as far as that corresponds to the rules of Etsy.

The description text should be well-structured and easily understandable. It is also important to mention dimensions if necessary. In order to avoid misunderstandings, a clear display of what the buyer gets for his money is recommended.

Always give priority to the benefit for the buyer.

The following structure has proved successful:

- The first two lines also appear in the Google link description. They increase the traffic if the offer is »put straight« there.

- Use bullet points and short sections in order to make it easier for the reader to get an overview.

- Show your enthusiasm for your products. Purely objective-technical texts do not fit the platform.

- Always argue from the customer's point of view. What does he get out of buying it? How will it change his life? ...

- Treat customers like friends. Speak of »I« and »we«.

It may make sense to offer various versions to the buyer. Those who for example sell clothes will want to offer them in different sizes and those who sell accessories perhaps want to offer their products in different colors. You have the choice. With that, different versions can have different prices.

Eventually, you can enter the tags and materials. Absolutely use these options. With that, you can dramatically increase your traffic.

Regarding tags Etsy recommends:

- Whom is it for?

- What is the main color?

- With which technique was is made?

- Which size does it have?

- What style is it?

- What is the main material?

- Does the item contain symbols or pictures?

- Do not forget to add synonyms. Buyers look for the same item in different kind of ways.

On Etsy, you can depict to where you ship for which conditions in a very explicit way. Use that option. For that, you can also add which costs incur for the shipping on single items as well as for the shipping of several items (combined shipping). Digital products (that can be downloaded) do not offer this possibility. Also, keep in mind that packaging is included in the calculation as well. You can add the respective costs to the product price or the shipping charges.

Customer loyalty on Etsy

On a big marketplace like Etsy customer loyalty is a central topic. If you want to be successful in the long run, your goal has to be to make your customers become your fans and friends that they appreciate you and your products and on the one hand, promote your products and on the other hand like to come back themselves to buy further products. That is the basis for your shop success.

For this you need to consider a few aspects:

Provide an excellent service.

It is not enough to simply send an item and a bill to your customers. That is what also marketplaces like Amazon do. You have to stand out by offering an extra in service to your customers. How this extra looks can vary depending on the area. Examples from experience:

- A seller of jewelry ships, in addition to the normal jewelry packaging, a nicely presented gift wrapper that allows the customer to easily give away the purchased jewelry.

- A manufacturer of soaps encloses a little heart-shaped soap with a new fragrance and a thank-you note, that also describes the fragrance of the new soap, in every order. Firstly, that

is for thanking for the order and pro-
motion for the next order.

- A seller of small wooden furniture, in
  addition, sends a small, beautifully de-
  signed brochure with care instruc-
  tions for the furniture as well as a
  sample of a beeswax care product
  (which he also sells by the way).

To an excellent customer service, of course,
also belongs to make the delivery deadline
and to respond to all messages within a
short time.

Put the customer in the center of your thinking

Get to know your customer. Many sellers
tend to always only think from the

perspective of their own products. Metaphorically speaking, they walk through their stock and put everything that is there in their shop. Truly successful salesmen change their perspective and observe their customer. They ask themselves what this person might need and how they could make their life more pleasant. From this, very different results can arise:

- Customer-friendly vending and packaging units

- Redesign of the products

- Compiling special offers (e.g. the beeswax care product for wooden furniture)

- Adjustment of the terms of shipment or packaging

- ...

Whatever might be your branch. If you think from the perspective of your customer and make your offers accordingly, you will have more satisfied customers and sooner or later also more customers.

Also, ask your customers for feedback and ask them what you could do better. Especially, if you give your customer the possibility to also make custom orders, you can learn a lot from them.

Always appreciate the concerns, suggestions and wishes of your customers. That does not mean that you have to realize every advise. In any case show that you appreciate the customers and their opinion. Those who tell you their opinion, show interest in your shop, even if they have not (yet) bought anything.

Social media - Success factor on Etsy

A wonderful possibility, on the one hand, in order to promote your own shop and on the other hand, in order to interact with customers, prospects and fans, is not only to connect your account with Twitter, Facebook and Google+, but also to build an interaction with your shop and other platforms, such as Pinterest and Tumblr. Social media is always also directly or indirectly a marketing platform. People that read the posts will potentially also want to learn more and will potentially visit your shop.

A possible strategy can for example be:

Both platforms can be wonderfully used for connecting with your customers. On there you can win new customers, join groups on the subject and also post news and thus gradually build your own community. But do not purely use your presence for advertisement. Put the topic in the center and not the products. Of course, you should also be present as a human. »People buy from people«.

Using Twitter

Post news about your topic. New offers also have a place on there, but here it applies as well: If it does not bring additional value to the customer to follow your tweets, he will not do that and probably also not retweet the tweets.

Using Tumblr

In German-speaking areas, Tumblr is still relatively small. Nevertheless, there are also already a few million users. The marketing expert Sebastian Merz has written a very informative book about how especially small companies and self-employed persons can ideally use this platform for marketing . The platform is a microblogging platform. It is a wonderful possibility to address potential customers with items, images, videos and other information on your topic and to win them with convincing information.

Using Pinterest

Pinterest: however, a platform that is still relatively sparsely used in our language area. Sebastian Merz has also written a book about that, which shows how the platform can optimally be used for marketing. Pinterest provides virtual pin boards on which people can pin images and videos on various topics. Nothing can be said against also displaying your products on a pin board and to link your shop and the respective item on it as well. This will not only increase your ranking in Google's search engine but also attract additional customers. Of course, you should also repin posts from others and thus build a network where posts are also re-pinned and with that can be spread virally.

.

There are endless other possibilities to inter-act with customers and prospects. This can be in the form of other social media plat-forms or also with classic e-mail marketing. What applies in any case: rather use a limited number of channels, that you use intensively and specifically than to own a dozen chan-nels on which »nothing goes«.

Etsy and Google SEO

The cheapest way to get people to visit your shop on the internet is undoubtedly a good listing on Etsy and Google.

In order to be found optimally, we already implemented the following points in the course of the book:

- Keyword - search and analysis

- Using keywords in the definition of the shop (name, title, announcements...)

- Using keywords in the item description (title, description, tags)

- Convincing first two lines on the item descriptions

- Names of the uploaded photographs

- Selecting the suitable shop category

- Involvement in social media, linked messages that provide the reader/viewer with additional value and thus are spread

- Links on other websites leading to your shop. If you operate an own homepage, Facebook page, etc., also post links to your shop.

Use the Etsy network

Different from many other market platforms, there is no »hewing and stabbing« between the providers on Etsy. Everyone rather healthily competes for customers. Besides that, many forms of cooperation between the sellers exist, which is also supported by the fact that many of them share common values and attitudes to life. Thus, one can speak of a real Etsy salesmen community.

There are several forms to start an interaction. Besides the obvious possibilities to directly message other sellers and the forum, there is also the possibility to »favor« the shops and thus perhaps be perceived by their operators. But even if that is not the case: every favorite note also leads to the shop of the respective operator and thus leads to additional links and a higher ranking in the Etsy search engine.

Besides that, there is the possibility to create team pages, where several operators chose an additional shared public image. Such team pages are usually topic-oriented (hand-made fishing baits and fishing rots) or geography-oriented. With that, you will also achieve a higher attention and presence and will possibly also get to know interesting people in your category.

Captains' Quarters
We'd like all the team captains to join us here

1946 Mitglieder

The Mods
We moderate the Etsy Forums

15 Mitglieder

Etsy Labs in Brooklyn, NY
Craft Nights are free (with RSVP), structured classes open to the public. Check the Event Calendar for upcoming dates!

1329 Mitglieder

Meet the Etsy Admin
One Admin, two Admin, see the list grow! We are a group dedicated to collecting all the folks who make Etsy tick from the inside out.

151 Mitglieder

Oberlin on Etsy
Here is a home for all you Obies on Etsy!

16 Mitglieder

Etsy Success
Sellers Unite!

52068 Mitglieder

Epilog

This book - is to my knowledge the first one on the topic Etsy that was also published in German - has hopefully given you a good insight into Etsy and its possibilities. Especially for »creative persons« the marketplace offers a first-class possibility to live from what you love.

I hope that I have made you curious and that my explanation can help you to make many positive experiences on Etsy as a seller.

Yours, Olav Kalt